SURVIVAL AND CHANGE

Holly Wallace

Heinemann
LIBRARY

www.heinemann.co.uk
Visit our website to find out more information about Heinemann Library books.

To order:
 Phone 44 (0) 1865 888066
 Send a fax to 44 (0) 1865 314091
 Visit the Heinemann Bookshop at www.heinemann.co.uk to browse our catalogue and order online.

First published in Great Britain by Heinemann Library, Halley Court, Jordan Hill, Oxford OX2 8EJ a division of Reed Educational and Professional Publishing Ltd. Heinemann is a registered trademark of Reed Educational & Professional Publishing Ltd.

OXFORD MELBOURNE AUCKLAND
JOHANNESBURG BLANTYRE GABORONE
IBADAN PORTSMOUTH (NH) USA CHICAGO

Designed by Celia Floyd
Originated by Dot Gradations
Printed in Hong Kong/China

ISBN 0 431 10921 4
05 04 03 02 01
10 9 8 7 6 5 4 3 2 1

British Library Cataloguing in Publication Data

Wallace, Holly
  Survival and change. – (Living things)
  1. Evolution (Biology) – Juvenile literature 2. Adaptation (Biology) – Juvenile literature 3. Competition (Biology) – Juvenile literature
  I. Title
  576.8

Acknowledgements

The Publishers would like to thank the following for permission to reproduce photographs:

Mary Evans Picture Library: pg.28; *Natural History Museum London*: pg.23, pg.26, M Long pg.23; *NHPA*: pg.6, MI Walker pg.4, Trevor McDonald pg.5; AP Barnes pg.7, Jean-Louis Le Moigne pg.7, pg.16, Andy Rouse pg.8, Stephen Krasemann pg.9, Lady Philippa Scott pg.11, Daniel Heuclin pg.12, Daryl Balfour pg.13, A.N.T. pg.13, David Woodfall pg.14, Karl Switak pg.15, Mirko Stelzner pg.17, Martin Harvey pg.18, Stephen Dalton pg.19, T Kitchin & V Hurst pg.20, Norbert Wu pg.21, pg.27, pg.27 Kevin Schafer pg.22, Anthony Bannister pg.25, NA Callow pg.28; *Oxford Scientific Films*: Liz & Tony Bomford pg.7, JAL Cooke pg.11, Rafi Ben-Shahar pg.15, Doug Allan pg.24, Konrad Wothe pg.26; *Planet Earth Pictures*: Peter Scoones pg.25.

Cover photograph reproduced with permission of Tony Stone.

Every effort has been made to contact copyright holders of any material reproduced in this book. Any omissions will be rectified in subsequent printings if notice is given to the Publisher.

Any words appearing in the text in bold, **like this**, are explained in the glossary.

Contents

Introduction

The six books in this series explore the world of living things. *Survival and Change* looks at how plants and animals appeared on Earth. It shows how they have changed over time and how they are still changing to give them a better chance of survival.

Long ago

Millions of years ago, the world looked very different. Fiery volcanoes covered the Earth. There were no living things. Over time, the seas filled with life, such as worms and jellyfish. Then plants began to grow on land and animals, such as dinosaurs, ruled the Earth. Finally, human beings appeared about 2 million years ago. We know about the plants and animals that lived on Earth from **fossils** in the rocks. Parts of dead plants and animals, such as bones, teeth and wood, were buried by sand and mud. They slowly turned to stone.

All change

Fossils and other clues show that the Earth is always changing. At times, steamy swamps grew on Earth. At other times, it was covered in ice. As the Earth changed, living things changed too. They had to cope with the new conditions, or die out. This led to the great variety of plants and animals we have today.

Fungi feed on other living things which can be alive or dead. All living things need food to survive.

Survival skills

A **habitat** is a place where a plant or animal lives. Habitats include mountains, deserts, rivers and forests. Living things have special features to help them survive in their habitat:

- Mountain yaks have long, thick coats to keep them warm.
- Limpets cling to seashore rocks with their strong tube-like feet to stop them being swept away by the tides.
- Lantern fish glow to find **prey** or a **mate** in the dark deep sea.

Plaice can change colour to blend in with the seabed. This is called **camouflage**.

Did you know?
The first living things probably grew about 3000 million years ago. Fossils of tiny **cells** have been found in ancient rocks.

Many kinds of life

How many different kinds of living things have you seen today? A pet cat or dog? Garden trees and flowers? Birds or butterflies in the sky? Worms in the soil? A spider hiding in the bathroom? And of course, people too. They are the most familiar living things of all.

Living things

There are millions of living things on Earth. Scientists sort them into groups. All the members in a group have certain features in common. A single kind of living thing is called a **species**. All the members of a species look very similar to each other. They can **breed** with each other. But they cannot breed with members of other species. Tigers, lions and leopards are all types of big cats. But they are all different species. Tigers have striped fur. Lions have fur that is yellow-brown, and leopards have fur with spots.

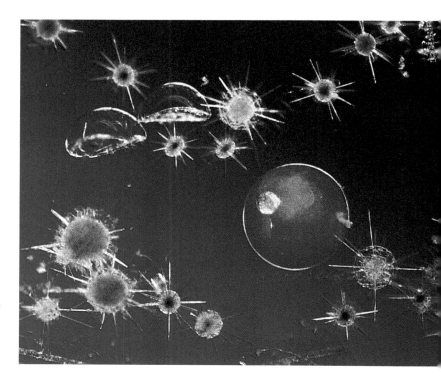

There might be more than 100 different species of tiny plants and animals in one drop of seawater.

Species features

There is an amazing **variety** of life on Earth. So far, scientists have discovered about two million different species. They include all kinds of animals and plants, **fungi** and tiny living things, such as **amoeba** and **bacteria**. They range in size from tiny one-**celled** plants to enormous whales. Each species has special features to help it survive in its home.

Did you know?

Insects are the largest group of living things. There are more than one million species. Beetles are the biggest group of insects. There are at least 250,000 species of beetles and probably many more.

Colorado beetle.

Cockchafer beetle.

Great diving beetle.

7

Different species

Grizzly bears live in North America. Brown bears live in Europe. Kamchatkan bears live in Asia. These three types of bears are different in size and fur colour. But their other features are all very similar. They can also **breed** with each other. This means they all belong to the same **species**. There are several other species of bear, for example the polar bear.

A grizzly bear.

Bear lifestyles

The gizzly bear, brown bear and Kamchatkan bear live in different places. But they all eat very similar food, make dens in the same way, raise their cubs in the same way and have similar enemies (mainly humans). They all follow similar lifestyles.

Grasshopper genes

It can be difficult to decide about species. Studying **genes** has helped scientists to find out that one species of grasshopper is in fact two species. The grasshoppers look the same but their genes are slightly different. Their songs are also different and they do not breed together.

Grass eaters

Zebras, gazelles and wildebeest are different species but they all live in the same place, on the African **grasslands**. They all eat grass. But they each eat different parts of the grass. Zebras eat longer grass. Wildebeest eat mid-length grass. Gazelles eat the shortest grass. This way they do not compete with each other for food.

Zebras and wildebeest grazing together on the African grasslands.

Battle for survival

Two species cannot live in the same place and eat exactly the same food. There would too much **competition** for food and shelter. One species would **adapt** better to the conditions. The other would die out, unless it changed too. This is why living things change all the time.

Did you know?
Baby eels are small, see-through and leaf-shaped. They look very different from adult eels. Scientists used to think that the babies and adults were two different eel species.

9

Survival

The best places for living things to survive are places with plenty of warmth, sunshine and water all year round. But even in the harshest places on Earth, such as dry deserts, dark ocean depths and icy **poles**, you find a great many living things. Life is very tough for them. They need special features and skills to stay alive.

Deep-sea survivors

Deep down in the ocean, the water is pitch black and cold. But thousands of fish and other creatures live in the ocean depths. Many deep-sea fish make their own light so that they can find their way in the dark. The light also helps them to find food, attract a **mate** and send signals to each other. Some deep-sea fish have very large mouths for swallowing food. It drifts down from the ocean surface. But food is scarce. The fish must make the most of any meal.

Freezing seas

Ice-fish live in the freezing seas around the poles. The water is always icy and cold. But the fish have a special **chemical** in their blood which stops them freezing solid. This is like the **anti-freeze** people use on their cars to stop them freezing. The chemical means that the fish can live in water which is so cold it would kill other creatures.

Cave birds

Oilbirds live in dark caves in South America. They spend their whole lives in darkness. To find their way around, they make lots of tiny, clicking sounds. Then they listen out for the echoes to tell how far they are from the cave walls.

A brine shrimp.

Salty water

Seawater contains small amounts of salt that do not harm living things. But too much salt can kill them. Some lakes are very salty. They contain ten times as much salt as the sea. Even so, creatures like brine shrimps live in the water.

An Arabian oryx.

Did you know?

The Arabian oryx is a type of antelope. It lives in the baking desert in the Middle East. Its body temperature can rise in the scorching midday Sun so that it does not get heatstroke. In the evening, it cools down again.

Unwelcome guests

There needs to be a good balance of **species** in a **habitat**. Otherwise, there would be too much **competition** for shelter and food. Usually, **predators**, disease and cold weather keep the species in check naturally. But sometimes the balance is upset, especially if a new species is brought in.

Rabbits everywhere

The common rabbit usually lives in south-west Europe and north-west Africa. But in about 1900, rabbits were introduced in Australia, too. They bred very quickly and became a pest. Now they eat farmers' crops and compete with local animals for food. They also weaken the ground with their burrows and spread diseases. In Europe and Africa, many rabbits were eaten by foxes, stoats and wild cats. But in Australia, they had very few enemies.

The prickly pear cactus grew out of control and upset the balance in its habitat.

Prickly pears

The prickly pear is a cactus. It was taken from America to Australia to grow into hedges. But it quickly grew out of control. Local animals could not eat it because of its sharp thorns.

Pests and pest control

In 1935, cane toads were brought from South America to Australia. Farmers wanted them to eat the sugar cane beetles that were ruining their crops. But the cane toads bred quickly and began to eat the local animals, such as ring-tailed possums and **cassowaries**. Some of these are now very rare. Cane toads have become serious pests, instead of being useful as pest controllers.

Under control

Many animals die from natural diseases. This helps to keep numbers under control. For example, **red-knee disease** has killed many frogs and toads in recent years.

Cane toads ooze poison that kills any animal that tries to eat it.

Did you know?

The water hyacinth grows very quickly and chokes up rivers and canals in Africa and Asia. It makes it difficult for boats to get through. The weed was brought from South America.

Water hyacinths in Lake Kariba, Zimbabwe, Africa.

Producing young

Members of one **species** only **breed** with others of their own species. This means that they produce young of their own species. They do not breed with other species. So a mother lion gives birth to baby lions. Seeds from a Scots pine tree grow into young Scots pines. But how does this happen? How do the parents pass their features on to their young?

Scots pines in the Cairngorms, Scotland.

Instructions for life

Each living thing grows according to a set of instructions called **genes**. They are quite like the plans for building a huge structure, such as a skyscraper. Genes are instructions for what living things look like and how they behave.

Passing on genes

Parents pass on their genes to their offspring when they breed. Many living things get half of their genes from their mother and half from their father. This is why they look like a mixture of their parents.

Genes in cells

Genes are found inside the **cells** of a living thing. They are coiled up tightly on long strings. Some living things are made of only one cell. Others, such as large trees or elephants, are made of millions of cells. Each cell in a human body contains more than 100,000 genes.

Baby lions and their mothers in Botswana, Africa.

Built-in behaviour

Genes tell living things how to behave in some situations. This is called **instinct**. For example, young ants clean and guard their nest and collect food without being taught how to do it. Baby lions know by instinct how to lie still if danger is near. Their genes carry instructions for this behaviour.

Did you know?

Many living things use **sexual reproduction**. This is when a male and a female parent breed together. Some living things use **asexual reproduction**. They split in two or put out a new shoot or stem. The new living thing looks exactly like its parent because it has exactly the same genes.

A creosote bush reproduces asexually.

Everyone is different

A huge flock of sea birds, such as gannets, may all look the same. But if you look closer, you will see that the birds are all slightly different. Some are bigger than others. Some have longer beaks or wider wings. In nature, even tiny differences are important. They give some of the birds a better chance of survival than others.

These gannets may all look the same. But they are all slightly different.

Gannet genes

Part of the reason why living things are different is because of their **genes**. All the gannets are the same **species**. They all have similar genes. But their genes are not exactly the same. There are two reasons why.

Mixing genes

The young gets half of its genes from its father and half of its genes from its mother. The genes get mixed during **breeding**. So each young gets a **unique** set of genes. This means that it is the only living thing with that particular mixture of genes.

Changing genes

Some genes get changed as they pass from the parents to the young. So they are not exact copies. Sometimes the changed genes mean that the young are a slightly different colour, shape or size. It may mean changes inside their bodies. The change may be helpful or harmful to a living thing.

Garden flowers

Genes are not the only reason why living things from the same species look different from each other. Flowers that grow in the shade of a tree may not be as tall and healthy as flowers that grow in the Sun.

Garden flowers.

Did you know?

Young produced by **asexual reprodution** have **identical** genes (see page 15). So do identical twins. They are born when one **egg** splits in two and each half grows into a baby. The twins look exactly the same.

Only some survive

Living things have to battle to survive. Sometimes different **species** compete with each other for shelter and food. Sometimes the battle is between members of the same species. Only those who **adapt** better to the conditions will survive.

Wild boars

Wild boars live in forests in Europe and Asia. A mother boar can have up to ten babies a year. This means that she could have 100 babies in her lifetime. If this happened, the world would be full of wild boars. But not all the young survive.

Baby wild boars all look alike. But each one has slightly different genes. This can make the difference between life and death.

The struggle for life

Baby wild boars have many enemies. They are eaten by leopards, wolves and hawks. The boars that survive may have a new feature which gives them a better chance of survival. This is passed down in their **genes**. For example, one boar might have a slightly different pattern of stripes on its coat. This helps to hide it in the undergrowth so that its enemies cannot see it.

Strong features

The baby boar with the best **camouflage** is most likely to survive, grow up and have young of its own. It passes on its camouflage genes to its young. This gives them a better chance of survival. Over many years, more and more wild boars get the camouflage genes. The whole species changes slightly.

Other changes

Many changes happen naturally. But people change species, too. Long ago, people picked out the tamest wild boars and the ones with the most meat. They bred them together. Over thousands of years the boars changed. Their **descendants** are farm pigs.

Evolution

This type of change happens in all living things. It is called **evolution**. It means that species get new features which give them a better chance of surviving.

Did you know?

Some plants eat meat. The Venus fly-trap waits until a fly lands on its leaves. Then it snaps its leaves shut. It **dissolves** the fly with special juices. This feature helps fly-traps to live in places with poor soil where other plants cannot grow.

New species

Tree shrews are small **mammals** that look like a cross between squirrels and shrews. But they belong to their own group. They live in the forests of South and East Asia. They eat insects, worms, seeds and fruit. There are eighteen different **species** of tree shrews. But all the species look alike and live in similar ways. How did this happen?

Splitting up

Imagine a big forest with one species of tree shrew. Gradually the forest gets split up. A new river forms after heavy rain and splits the forest in two. Then a huge fire burns, dividing it up even more. There are now several small patches of forest, with some of the tree shrews in each.

New species

The tree shrews are all still the same species. But slowly conditions in each new patch of forest change. The tree shrews change too, to suit their surroundings. Soon, the single species of tree shrew splits into several new species. They look alike and live in similar ways but they cannot **breed** with each other.

Different tree shrew species look alike because long ago they were all one species.

Splitting species

Over time, one species can change and split into two or more species, like the tree shrews. In this way, many new species have appeared on Earth over millions of years. They look alike because they are closely related. That is why, today, there is such an amazing **variety** of living things in the world.

Evolving eels

Garden eels live in burrows on the seabed. They have split into many different species. This is because some live in warm or cold seas, or in deep or shallow water. The garden eels had to change as conditions in the sea changed. Otherwise they would not have survived.

Garden eels in the warm Caribbean Sea.

Charles Darwin

Charles Darwin (1809–1882) was a famous British scientist. He wrote a book called *On the Origin of Species*. In it, Darwin explained how **evolution** works. He also suggested that human beings were evolved from apes. At the time, people were very angry. Today, we know that he was right.

Prehistoric life

Over millions of years, new **species** have evolved on Earth. But other species have died out. Many of the species that once lived on Earth have disappeared (see page 4). We know that they existed from **fossils** and other clues.

Earliest life

Scientists think that the first living things on Earth were tiny, single **cells**. They lived about 3000 million years ago. They were too small to see except under a microscope. The first plants and animals lived in the sea about 1000 million years ago. The animals included jellyfish and worms.

Land and sea

The first animals with shells lived in the sea about 570 million years ago. They were **trilobites**, **ammonites** and lampshells. About 500 million years ago, the first fish swam in the seas. By 350 million years ago, sharks like the ones we have today appeared. The first plants grew on land about 400 million years ago, followed by the first land animals such as millipedes, insects and **reptiles**.

A trilobite fossil.

Did you know?
Trilobites were ancient cousins of crabs and prawns. Many fossils have been found of their hard shells.

Dinosaur days

The most famous ancient animals were the mighty dinosaurs. They first lived on Earth about 230 million years ago. The earliest **mammals** appeared at about the same time. They were small and looked like shrews. Reptiles with wings called pterosaurs flew in the air. Fish-like reptiles called ichthyosaurs swam through the seas.

The first bird, *Archaeopteryx*, lived 150 million years ago.

Sudden changes

About 65 million years ago, a great change happened on Earth. Many kinds of plants and animals died out. They included dinosaurs and ichthyosaurs. No one knows exactly why. Some scientists think that a giant **meteorite** crashed into the Earth. It caused a thick dust cloud that blocked out the Sun and made the Earth icy cold. After this, mammals and birds quickly increased in numbers.

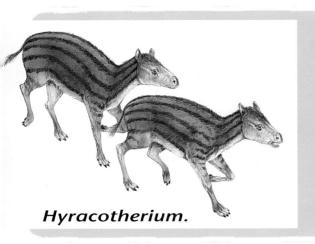

Hyracotherium.

Bigger and faster

Horses have become bigger. *Hyracotherium* was an early horse that lived 50 million years ago. It was no bigger than a rabbit. *Mesohippus* lived 30 million years ago. It was the size of a dog. Getting bigger meant horses could run faster, away from **predators**.

Then and now

Fossils in the rocks show us that most living things have changed over time. But a few kinds of living things have stayed the same. Some of the **species** we have today are very like those that lived millions of years ago. They are sometimes called 'living fossils'. But how have they survived for so long without changing?

Good design

Sometimes nature designs a living thing so well first time that it does not need to change. It can cope with many changing conditions. For example, sharks first lived about 350 million years ago. They look much the same today.

Safe surroundings

Some living things do not change because their **habitat** does not change. They have no new dangers to face. Lampshells first lived about 570 million years ago. They lived in the mud on the ocean floor. They still live there today. They look the same because their habitat is still very much the same.

Lampshells on the ocean floor have hardly changed for millions of years.

Slow change

The velvet worm lives on the rainforest floor, among the rotting leaves. It looks like a cross between a worm and a millipede. Velvet worms have hardly changed since they first lived on Earth 550 million years ago. Species that change slowly may be able to cope better when the conditions change than species that change very quickly.

A velvet worm.

Did you know?
Scientists thought that a fish called a coelacanth died out over 50 million years ago. But, in 1938, a live coelacanth was caught in the Indian Ocean. It was a living fossil.

A coelacanth.

Ancient trees
Fossils of gingko trees date back more than 100 million years. This ancient tree was thought to be **extinct**. But scientists found it growing in China. Today, you can find gingko trees in parks and gardens around the world.

The same but different

At first sight sharks and dolphins look alike. If you saw them swimming together in the sea, it might be difficult to tell them apart. They both have similar body shapes and curved fins on their backs. But they belong to two very different groups of animals. Sharks are kinds of fish. Dolphins are kinds of **mammals**. So why do they look much the same?

Looking the same

Many large sea creatures, such as sharks, dolphins and whales look similar because they have the same problem to solve – how to swim through the sea. They all have a smooth, **streamlined** body shape. This makes it easier to cut through the water. They also have fins or flippers and tails for pushing themselves along and steering through the water. They are different animals with similar shapes.

A dolphin's smooth shape helps it to swim fast.

An ichthyosaur was an ancient **reptile** that lived in the sea. Its body shape was like a dolphin's.

Looking different

Sometimes living things that were closely related gradually look less alike. This happens if they live in different places and have different ways of life. Many fish use their fins for swimming. But mudskippers have arm-like fins for pulling themselves along on land. Lionfish have fan-like fins with poisonous spines for defending themselves from enemies. Remoras are tiny fish. They have a top fin shaped like a sucker for clinging on to a bigger creature, like a shark.

The lionfish's front fins are shaped like sharp spines.

A remora clinging on to a shark. The shark carries it through the sea.

Survival and change today

Human beings are changing the world very quickly. Farmers plant crops and raise animals. People build factories, mines, roads, towns and cities. Everywhere, wild spaces are being used up. Sometimes is it difficult for plants and animals to cope with all the changes.

Changing too fast

Extinction is when a living thing dies out for ever. It has happened many times in the past. But today, it is happening more quickly than ever before. Hundreds of **species** have already died out. They cannot cope with the way in which human beings are changing the Earth.

Wildlife in danger

Some rare animals, such as elephants and tigers, are killed for their tusks and fur coats. Others are hunted for sport. Some, such as parrots and monkeys, are collected for pets or for zoos. Precious plants, such as orchids, are taken from the wild too. All these things are putting wildlife around the world in great danger.

About 1000 years ago, a giant bird called the moa lived in New Zealand. But so many moas were hunted and killed that today they are extinct.

Helping wildlife

All over the world, the **habitats** of living things are being destroyed. People are cutting down forests and digging up meadows to make space for farms, towns, shopping centres and factories. Often the plants and animals that live there cannot find another place to live. Then they become extinct. The best way we can help them is to stop the damage and start putting things right again.

In some places bumblebees have become very rare. This is because the flowers they feed on have been sprayed with poisonous **chemicals**. The flowers die and so do the bees.

Did you know?

Some types of tourism are helping wildlife. People pay to watch rare animals, such as whales and gorillas. They do not disturb the animals and the money they pay helps to protect local wildlife.

Captive breeding

Some species are so rare that only a few creatures survive in the wild. Now these animals are being **bred** in zoos and wildlife parks. Then their young are put back into the wild. This has happened to golden lion tamarins and Californian condors.

Glossary

adapt   having a special feature that helps an animal or plant survive in its habitat

ammonites   prehistoric sea creatures, related to cuttlefish and squid. They had shells coiled in a spiral.

amoeba   tiny, one-celled living thing that lives in water

anti-freeze   a substance used to stop something freezing, for example, car windscreens

asexual reproduction   when a living thing reproduces from just one parent. The parent splits in two, or part of the parent buds or splits off, to make a new living thing.

bacteria   tiny living things that are found almost everywhere

breed   to produce new living things

camouflage   having a special shape, colour or pattern that helps a living thing blend in with its surroundings

cassowary   a large bird which cannot fly

cell   a tiny building block that makes up the bodies of all living things

chemical   a substance found as a solid, liquid or gas

competition   when living things struggle with each other for food, shelter and mates

descendants   relatives of living things that lived long ago

dissolve   to turn into liquid

egg   a special cell made by a female animal. It joins with a male sperm cell to make a new living thing.

evolution   how living things change and adapt over time to be better suited to surviving in their habitat

extinct, extinction   when a living thing dies out for ever

fossil   the remains of an ancient living thing that has turned to stone over millions of years

fungi   living things such as mushrooms, toadstools and mould. Fungi are not animals or plants.

genes   instructions in a living thing's cells that say what a living thing will look like and how it will behave

grasslands huge, open spaces covered in grass and bushes

habitat a particular place where plants and animals live

identical exactly the same

instinct when a living thing knows how to behave or do a particular task without having to be taught

mammals animals such as elephants, bats, horses and humans. They feed their babies on milk.

mate a partner to produce young with

meteorite a huge lump of space rock that crashes into the Earth

poles two regions at the north and south ends of the Earth. They are the North Pole and the South Pole.

predator an animal that hunts and kills other animals for food

prey animals that are hunted and killed for food

red-knee disease a disease that harms an amphibian's skin and breathing. It is caused by a fungus.

reptiles animals with scaly skin that live on land. They include snakes, lizards and dinosaurs.

sexual reproduction when a living thing needs two parents, one male and one female, to make more of itself. Each make special cells which must join together to make a new cell. This grows into a living thing.

species a group of living things that have certain features in common and can breed together

streamlined having a smooth shape for cutting through the air or water

trilobites prehistoric sea creatures. They looked a bit like large woodlice.

unique the only one of its kind

variety a large range and number of something, such as living things

Index